ISBN 9798345148945

POO - DOLF
THE
Farting
Reindeer

Gusty Maguire

Poo-dolf the farting reindeer

Had a very gassy rear

And if you
ever saw it

You had better
just steer clear!

All of the
other reindeer

Used to see his
butt and run

They wouldn't
be near Poo-dolf

Any time his
farts begun

Then one soggy
Christmas Eve

Santa came
to say

"Poo-dolf with your
farts so strong,

Won't you pull
my sleigh along!"

Then all the
reindeer loved him!

They didn't have
to work at all

Poo-dolf the
farting reindeer

With his farts
they'd never fall!

Merry

Christmas!